THE
MIRACLES
OF JESUS

THE MIRACLES
OF JESUS

*Meditations
and Prayers*
FOR LENT

WESSEL BENTLEY

UPPER
ROOM BOOKS®
NASHVILLE

THE MIRACLES OF JESUS
Meditations and Prayers for Lent
© 2012 by Wessel Bentley
All rights reserved.

Cover design: Bruce Gore/Gorestudio.com
Cover photo: © Arnold Friberg, photograph courtesy of Friberg Fine Art, Inc.

LIBRARY OF CONGRESS CATALOGING-IN-PUBLICATION DATA

Bentley, Wessel.
    The miracles of Jesus: meditations and prayers for Lent / Wessel Bentley.
        p. cm.
    ISBN 978-0-8358-1113-2—ISBN 978-0-8358-1121-7—ISBN 978-0-8358-1172-9
    1. Jesus Christ—Miracles—Meditations. 2. Lent—Prayers and devotions. I. Title.
    BT366.3.B47 2012
    232.9'55—dc23

                                                    2011051677

Printed in the United States of America

CONTENTS

THE GOSPEL OF MARK
Getting to Know Jesus During Lent

THE GOSPEL OF MATTHEW
Getting to Know Jesus in Our Faith

THE GOSPEL OF LUKE
Getting to Know Jesus of the Marginalized

THE GOSPEL OF JOHN
Getting to Know Jesus Who Brings Life

ACKNOWLEDGMENTS

Writing a book is a team effort. Through the years, the teams at Upper Room Ministries and Africa Upper Room Ministries have showed tremendous dedication and professionalism in my dealings with them. Thank you to each and every one! Special thanks must go to Rita Collett, who not only did a sterling job at improving the readability of the manuscript but challenged my thinking on countless occasions. Similarly, I must thank Roland Rink and Renny Stoltz for their ongoing support and motivation. Most of all, I extend appreciation to my family, who encourage me daily to be the best father and husband I can be.

I dedicate this book to our son,

Nathan

who helps us appreciate life
from more angles than the obvious.
You are a gift!

INTRODUCTION

*L*ENT IS A PREPARATORY TIME of forty days before Easter. Our journey starts on Ash Wednesday when we are reminded of our mortality and sin. Our cluttered lives often crowd out the reminders that Ash Wednesday brings. Activities, responsibilities, and even dreams or anxieties may shape the way we see ourselves and form the way we live out this miraculous gift of life.

On Ash Wednesday we cut to the core of our existence. We are not what we eat. We are not what we do. We are not what we fear. We are human beings, created in the image of God; but we have accumulated all kinds of complexities that make our core identity, at times, hard to find.

Easter brings new beginnings, so during Lent we undergo a process of letting go. We may find that letting go is not as easy as it seems. Letting go of things like addictions or luxuries makes us feel uncomfortable; it may take a miracle for us to experience relief.

During this Lenten time we will focus on Jesus' miracles, complex events that not only touched people through healing, multiplication, or resurrection but challenged attitudes and beliefs. This complexity makes Jesus' miracles timeless, for they can touch people's lives today just as they did nearly two thousand years ago.

We will take this Lenten journey day by day, so I encourage you to spend time with the scripture readings, meditations, and with God. Allow God to speak and show you what you need to let go of. You may even decide to give something up during Lent—a fast. Choose one activity, one luxury, or one item that will require effort on your part to give up during this time. Don't simply give it up, but use it differently. You may choose to fast thirty minutes of sleep and spend that time in meditation. You may choose to drink water with your lunch rather than a soft drink. Put that money aside, and use it to enrich someone else's life. Fasting teaches us that many things we take for granted are indeed luxuries or gifts.

Viewing these aspects of our lives enables us to thank God for other parts of our lives that go unnoticed. We become aware of people for whom the lack or absence of this gift is a daily reality. So during these forty days we try to strip ourselves of "things" that hinder our relationship with God or neighbor. We devote more time to God; with Easter's arrival, we will truly be able to start afresh.

One last note: If you find it difficult to give something up and slip along the way, don't stop. Try again. God's love and grace are far greater than your attempt to be perfect. I invite you on this journey.

HOW TO USE THIS BOOK

*T*HE MEDITATIONS IN THIS BOOK begin on Ash Wednesday and end on Easter Sunday. Each day starts with a scripture reading, followed by a meditation. You will notice that the meditations are not a scholarly exegesis of each passage. In preparing these meditations, I asked myself the question: "By studying this miracle, what insight do I gain about how God wants to heal us today?" The meditations are therefore contemplative, and I invite you to listen to what God may be saying to you through these texts. Some questions or suggestions for reflection follow each meditation. Take the suggestions seriously; answer the questions honestly. Perhaps write down some thoughts as you engage in this time of inner conversation. "Focus for today," which follows, will aid you in exploring opportunities for healing in a practical way, based on the thoughts of the meditation. Finally, each meditation closes with a prayer. Remember at least one aspect of the day's meditation as you enter your daily journey. Make the meditations relevant to your life as well as to the lives of those around you.

I have structured the meditations around the miracles recorded in the different Gospels. Each section will describe an aspect of the Lenten journey associated with each Gospel. Some sections are longer than others as the different Gospel writers accorded varied levels of importance to the miracles performed by Jesus.

I provide written meditations for every day from Monday to Friday. You may use Saturday to reflect on the previous week's journey and then join in worship with a Christian community on Sunday, taking the traditional Lenten rest. The first week, however, is a partial week; begin with Day 1 on Ash Wednesday. The final meditation is offered on Easter Sunday to celebrate Jesus' resurrection and the conclusion of the Lenten journey. I hope that when that day comes, you can acknowledge a definite death to self and a resurrection to new life in Christ.

THE GOSPEL OF MARK

Getting to Know Jesus During Lent

MARK INTRODUCES JESUS to an audience of
people who may not have heard of him before. His
audience consists largely of Gentiles—non-Jews. By
placing a high importance on the miracles, Mark
tries to convince his readers that Jesus was a man
like no other. He was the Son of God! Probably the
first Gospel account in our Bibles to be written, the
words Mark records invite us to get to know this
Jesus who has the authority and power to touch
lives and bring restoration to those who seek God.

DAY 1 † ASH WEDNESDAY

Jesus, who confronts demons

📖 Read Mark 1:23-26

*T*HESE VERSES RECOUNT the first miracle recorded in the Gospel According to Mark. Of the many miracles related to demon exorcism, this story is unique. The man is in the synagogue, among the worshipers. While there the man asks Jesus this question: "What have you to do with us, Jesus of Nazareth?" How many others, even religious people, will utter words similar to these in Jesus' years of ministry to come? The Pharisees and Sadducees regard Jesus with skepticism, their religious piety clouding their ability to recognize Jesus as the promised Messiah.

We may wonder, *What is this man doing in the synagogue?* The synagogue would seem a most unwelcoming place for demons. Yet Mark clearly notes that the demons' discomfort comes not from the location but from Jesus' presence. "Possession in the synagogue" makes for an interesting news headline. It encourages us to consider the demons we carry with us. We may be deluded in believing that membership in a church community or regular church attendance rids us of such things. But consider this: which demons do not feel threatened by our worship, the gathering of God's people? Sometimes we use religion to mask the presence of our own demons. Religious piety and the appearance of religious devotion to one greater than ourselves can easily become the playground for the evils of power, dominance, greed, lust, and many more.

We harbor no illusion that the church is devoid of its own demons. History tells us otherwise. This synagogue is not exempt from this historic truth. Yet, Jesus' presence clears this place of worship from its evil. More than that, the man experiences healing.

A great challenge during Lent arises when we pose the question as to whether we and our places and communities of worship, when confronted with Jesus' presence, respond with the words: "What have you to do with us, Jesus of Nazareth?" Mark invites us and our faith communities not to be deceived by the demons in our midst but to know the cleansing power of Jesus' voice.

Reflection

Where do your demons lie? What scandals have challenged your faith community? What within your place of worship has nothing to do with the person of Jesus Christ? Invite Jesus into those moments and places and pray for forgiveness, healing, and deliverance.

Focus for today

Pray for yourself and those in leadership positions in your congregation. Pray that God will enhance their ability to discern right from wrong and evil from righteousness. Be mindful of your own body as a place of worship.

Prayer

Lord, you command evil spirits, and they obey you. We know that we can harbor evil—even in our worship settings. Commanding God, speak into our lives and drive away the darkness so that we may live our lives and worship you in righteousness and in truth. Amen.

DAY 2 † THURSDAY

Jesus, who goes home with you

🕊 Read Mark 1:29-34

$\mathcal{M}$ARK RELATES THE STORY of Jesus' visit to the home of Simon and Andrew where Jesus heals Simon's mother-in-law. Jesus has just left worship at the synagogue and is on his way to Simon's home. Perhaps Simon has ulterior motives, knowing that his mother-in-law stands a chance of being healed that day.

Verse 29 offers a valuable lesson when it states, "They left the synagogue." Notice the way Jesus moves from one place to the other. We may interpret this verse as Jesus concluding one aspect of his day and moving on to the next as if the two aspects have no relation. We make compartmentalizing our lives a common practice. We seem to have a time and a place for everything: a time to go to work, a time to return home, a time to prepare a meal, and even a time for worship.

We often get upset when times and places get jumbled. We may tend to think that we meet God at church or during worship. God remains behind until we choose to return. But Simon does not leave God at the synagogue that day. He invites Jesus to go home with him. Upon Jesus' arrival, he touches and heals. Have you thought about the possibilities if you allow Jesus to go home with you or perhaps to join you at work?

We require healing of the idea that God resides at church and/or that God only speaks and touches us in times and places of worship. When we dare believe that God follows us out of church and accompanies us wherever we travel, it may surprise us to see the hand of God at work in both the matters we regard as unimportant and in the issues that we believe lie beyond anyone's control. Journey with this text throughout your day. As you move from one place to the next, invite Jesus to travel with you and to touch the people and situations that need him most.

Reflection

Jesus did not come to this world only to be worshiped in faith communities. Jesus journeyed with people and accepted people in the places where they were. Pray and invite Jesus to journey with you today. How would you feel if Jesus climbed into your car, accompanied you home, or went along to work?

Focus for today

Experience Jesus' presence each moment. Pray as you enter each new place, welcoming Christ to touch and to heal. Take note of those who may need Jesus' touch. Remind them that the miracle of Christ's presence moves beyond church to all situations.

Prayer

O God, we acknowledge that we often leave you behind at our place and time of meditation and devotion. Sometimes we even leave you at church. We invite you to join us at home and at work. Touch our lives and the lives of others in ways that we never expected. In Jesus' name. Amen.

DAY 3 † FRIDAY

Jesus, who makes clean

❧ Read Mark 1:40-44

*T*HE MAN'S DISEASE makes him ritually unclean. By law he cannot be in close contact with any "clean" person, since he might contaminate them. Notice the man's request. He not only asks for healing, which is implied in his request, but he asks Jesus to "make [him] clean." Besides healing from his disease, he wants to find acceptance and inclusion in the community.

Many stigmas and diseases exclude us from relationship. The exclusion may result from people's beliefs and biases. Think about your attitudes toward those who have a criminal record. What about those who come from foreign places, wanting to make a living and to create a home in your community? Do they find welcome, or are they treated as somehow "diseased"?

Sometimes our exclusion of others develops from our own sense of shame, guilt, or from terrible life experiences. Victims of sexual offenses or other forms of abuse often feel, so to speak, "ritually unclean."

Listen to what Jesus tells the man. Jesus desires his cleanness. More than that, Jesus wants the man to feel clean. Jesus touches him, pronounces him clean, and brings healing to his life. Then Jesus goes one step farther. He tells the man to go to the priest, the one who will pronounce him clean.

Jesus' healing of the man may foster the healing of prejudice. Imagine the man returning to the same priest who had declared him unclean and asking that he restore his dignity. We bring to Jesus that which makes us feel unclean. We allow Jesus to touch our lives and restore wholeness. After we receive this healing, we may engage those who carry prejudices. God may heal them too.

Reflection

Think about the ways you have made other people feel "ritually unclean" by deliberately excluding them. Bring your own prejudices and fears to God for healing.

Focus for today

Make an effort to reach out to persons you consider to be "different." Help them feel included and loved; affirm their dignity and self-worth.

Prayer

Almighty God, make us clean. We place ourselves in your hands, trusting in your grace to make us whole. Open our eyes to see those who feel excluded by their communities and ours. May we be instruments of your hands, speaking and performing healing in places of abandonment. In Jesus' name we pray. Amen.

DAY 4 † SATURDAY

Reflect on this past week and write down some new insights into your own need for Jesus' presence in your life.

What demons have you been carrying around, and how has Jesus threatened their presence this week?

How has inviting Jesus to be part of your everyday journey changed your outlook on living a Christian life?

How has Jesus made you clean? How has Jesus used you to help others feel included and worthy of God's love?

DAY 5 † MONDAY

Jesus, who heals hurts and sins

🕊 Read Mark 2:3-12

*F*OUR PEOPLE BRING the paralytic to Jesus for healing, not for forgiveness of sin.[1] Jesus' proclamation may seem completely out of place to us; but to the people in Jesus' context, his statement made sense. A common belief held that sin and misfortune went hand-in-hand. A sinful life would manifest in ill health, poverty, and adversity. The righteous would experience wealth, wisdom, and abundance. The man's "friends" probably bring him to Jesus for the removal of his paralysis, but they also want Jesus to take away the "curse" of his misfortune. Jesus does not disappoint.

Jesus addresses the root of the man's problems: "Son, your sins are forgiven." Can we imagine the man's relief? Even if he remains paralyzed for the rest of his life, he rests assured of God's love and acceptance.

In our day and age, we distinguish between sin and suffering. We do not equate suffering with divine punishment of our sins. However, we need not dismiss this miracle simply because we do not adhere to that ancient belief. Consider the following: When we go to God for healing, do we want God merely to treat the symptoms? God speaks to more than what we present as our "ailments." God speaks to the root of our being. God offers holistic healing, the transformation of our entire lives!

As a minister, I often see how God brings healing to people's lives. In most cases, people receive more healing than they bargained for. God heals the body, relationships, self-image—perhaps even our outlook on life. During Lent, as we present ourselves for healing, may we allow God to dig a bit deeper and touch the areas that matter most.

Reflection

What have you been praying for? What deeper issues might God need to address before resolving your "surface" request?

Focus for today

Make every effort in your time of prayer to bring all matters to God, including the hidden hurts of your life. Allow God to speak into them, and trust that divine wisdom guides God's healing.

Prayer

O Lord, we bring our hurts, fears, and life situations before you. We acknowledge that you see deeper and know more clearly; therefore, help us graciously accept your work of healing, affirming that you treat more than the symptoms. Amen.

DAY 6 † TUESDAY

Jesus, who reaches beyond taboos

🌿 Read Mark 3:1-5

*I*S IT LAWFUL TO DO GOOD or to do harm on the sabbath, to save life or to kill?" Think about this question for a minute. The miracle seems to hinge on this question in which Jesus juxtaposes his intentions with those of the Pharisees. Jesus wants to heal and bring life, while the Pharisees watch and wait for an opportunity to accuse him of wrongdoing and so orchestrate his downfall.

The Pharisees simply do not get it. This is one of many sabbath miracles in the Bible where Jesus confronts a dilemma of whether or not to heal. The Pharisees clearly interpret the law as forbidding *any* work on the sabbath, even if the action would help someone in need. How does the man with the withered hand feel? We can imagine his conflicting emotions. His opportunity for healing comes under the Pharisees' glaring and judgmental eyes.

We acknowledge that the law has its place, but sometimes becoming slaves to the law strips people of the opportunity for wholeness. I have heard people claim that they no longer go to church because they cannot afford to tithe. Others refuse to worship when a female preacher leads the service. They base their decision on biblical texts.

Jesus does not abolish the law but fulfills it. I challenge us this day to offer our legalistic concerns to Christ. Instead of holding on to our pain for the sake of pride and piety, we can allow Jesus to touch, to heal, and to transform perspectives and bring healing to our lives. We do not throw the law out the window. Jesus understood the emphasis of the spirit of the law: a focus on personal wholeness rather than personal righteousness. No work on the sabbath created a space for people to refrain from work in order to worship, to commune with others, and to appreciate God's gift of life. Jesus reveals God's power by touching this man's life, and the man experiences a new form of wholeness.

Reflection

Consider the legalistic attitudes and perspectives held by some church people. What examples come to your mind as to how these attitudes and perspectives have denied others Christian love?

Focus for today

Take some time today to think through your own addiction to the law. Does it save life or kill?

Prayer

Loving God, we sometimes use your word to justify our narrow-mindedness. We use it to veil our fears and anxieties. May we discover the fullness of the life you offer despite the ways we apply law to our lives. For this reason we pray for wisdom. In Jesus' name. Amen.

DAY 7 † WEDNESDAY

Jesus, who is in control

🕊 Read Mark 4:35-41

*I*T SEEMS TO BE a good day for sailing. Nothing in the text indicates a brewing storm or any second thoughts of the disciples about going out onto the lake. What might have been the disciples' response to the invitation to travel "to the other side," if they had known what awaited them?

If we had been part of the crowd by the sea, our foreknowledge of the coming storm would have allowed us to remain behind, pitch a tent, and share a meal while waiting for better conditions. But life is not that predictable.

Although some of the disciples are seasoned sailors, even they cannot predict what will take place within the next few hours. Such assurance and control over their environment would have saved them tremendous anxiety.

The power of prediction nevertheless robs us of life, and this robber has become part of modern living! We actually welcome the robber. Predictability offers a sense of control over circumstances that await us in the future. The question that draws our attention to healing today is this: "Do you know what awaits you today?" Sometimes we fare better not knowing.

The good news of this miracle comes in the midst of the fearful events; the disciples receive assurance of the Lord's presence. He stands and rebukes the storm while the disciples are petrified with fear. This miracle also involves healing—the healing of people's hearts in admitting that they are not the masters of their own destinies, owners and directors of their experiences. If we join the disciples on this journey, the experience will unmask the control we assume over our own lives and enable us to surrender to the direction of Jesus. He speaks on our behalf when life seems uncontrollable, unpredictable, and violent.

Reflection

Recall a time in your life when you would have chosen not to have a particular event form part of your life story. How did you experience God's presence in that situation?

Focus for today

Life might surprise you today. When facing moments of uncertainty, anxiety, or fear, pray for God's guidance and authority.

Prayer

Almighty God, every moment is unique. As you travel with us through the day, we depend on your presence and your voice, which calms every storm. Heal us, O God, of our need to control all things. Amen.

DAY 8 † THURSDAY

Jesus, who restores identities

📖 Read Mark 5:1-15

"WHAT HAVE YOU TO DO with me, Jesus?" Can you sense the extent to which this man has surrendered himself to self-destruction? The community has no place for him. Its members bind him whenever they manage to get hold of him. His only company is the dead. At least *they* aren't out to get him.

Jesus' visit is different from any the man has previously experienced. Rather than trying to catch and shackle him, Jesus wants to free him. Rather than cursing and swearing at him, Jesus asks his name. This man with no place in society meets another who knows about this way of being.

Jesus not only wants to disperse the man's demons; he desires wholeness for this man. In this miracle, a radical transformation takes place. Jesus delivers him from demon-possession and gives back his dignity. Now the man can once again reside among the living. Instead of being called "Legion" or "Mob," he probably got the name back that his parents called him at birth.

This Lenten season can bring change in our lives. Jesus' loving presence exposes the hidden places of our being. Naturally we ask, "What have you to do with me, Jesus?" Perhaps we expect Jesus to treat those hidden parts of our lives the same way others do. They bind, reject, and abandon us. But not Jesus. We let Jesus touch these parts of our lives with love. He gives us hope. Jesus can restore lives and heal our brokenness. We find our new identity in God's love.

Reflection

Recall the past hurts that have overtaken your life. How have these molded you as a person? Which hurts won't you let go of? Which hurts won't let go of you? Allow Jesus to speak into these areas of your life. Spend some time in prayer; name these issues; and surrender them to God.

Focus for today

Take careful note of people in your family or at work. Who is showing signs of being weighed down? Get to know their name. Pray for their healing throughout the day.

Prayer

Lord Jesus, what do you want with our hurts? We bind them close so no one can meddle with them. We thank you for your loving nature that looks at us with kindness and in compassion. Assure us that you know what to do with our brokenness. Amen.

DAY 9 † FRIDAY

Jesus, who crosses boundaries

🕊 Read Mark 5:22-24, 35-43

*H*AVE YOU EVER given up? We've all had those moments when an event or action seems inevitable, and we surrender to the outcome of a situation. Some may call it "making peace with" or "finding closure." The bearers of bad news come to share this point of no return with Jairus. According to them, it is all over. Nothing more can be done to save his daughter. He has to make peace with this event and move on with his life—now without his beloved child. Jesus surprises these realists. His command to the girl shows us that no situation lies beyond God's reach.

As a minister I have often returned from a hospital visit or sickbed thinking to myself that this person will not live long. On other occasions, I have looked at church budgets or counseled people and reached certain conclusions in my own mind about what would unfold. The surprise when God says, "I decide otherwise," always humbles. It draws us to our knees acknowledging that God's view is much more enlightened than our own.

This miracle reminds us of our own fallible beliefs and conclusions. In this Lenten journey God can surprise us with a few words: "Little girl, get up!" When all seems lost and beyond our control: "Get up!" When life offers the finality of a lost job, forgotten hope, failed marriage: "Get up!" These words, when spoken by the divine voice, silence the critics yet, no one can force or persuade God to perform this resurrection; these words come from God in God's own time.

Reflection

Recall moments when God surprised you with the expression, "I know better." How did you respond? What does it mean for you today that God knows better, even when you have made up your mind?

Focus for today

Consider your words today. Surrender yourself to the possibility that things may not be as fixed or absolute as you have imagined. Lent fosters an openness to being astonished by God's self-revelation.

Prayer

God of the living and of the dead, in our Christian faith we proclaim you as the God of resurrection. Not only did Christ conquer death, but he offers us the promise that all will rise to new life through you. You even respond to our needs, long dead and buried in human opinion, by bringing new life in all its fullness. We pray for resurrection today. Amen.

DAY 10 † SATURDAY

How has Jesus changed your life during this past week?

Jesus has forgiven your sins. He also addresses the root of personal struggle. What has Jesus been saying to you about forgiveness and your struggles this week?

Name your storms to which Jesus has brought peace.

How has God spoken healing into your lost causes?

DAY 11 † MONDAY

Jesus, who redeems by reputation

ॐ Read Mark 5:25-29

*T*HIS MIRACLE TAKES PLACE while Jesus is attending to someone else's need. Jesus has set out for Jairus's house. This desperate woman has consulted physicians far and wide but with no success. Then she hears about Jesus, no doubt from those who have witnessed his miraculous wonders. The text does not indicate that she comes to listen to Jesus or to hear the message of his good news. She comes to Jesus because of what she has heard about him. Verse 27, while seemingly insignificant in the greater scope of the story, is pivotal to the events that unfold in her life.

Some may say that the woman heard the testimonies about Jesus by coincidence. I prefer to view it as God's grace in action, a God-incidence, a miracle. Think about your own faith journey. How did you come to Jesus? Why did you come to Jesus? The woman's constant hemorrhaging would have left her tired and drained. Hearing about Jesus changes her life. You may know people who have turned from a drained existence to a life of healing, wholeness, and value through Jesus. This turnaround could easily result from their response to another's faith story.

When we share our faith stories—when we point to Jesus—they become instrumental in bringing about change in people's lives. Maybe we need to be healed from the belief that our faith stories are insignificant and not worth sharing. Our testimony, however spectacular or subtle, tells the story of God at work in our life. God can

use our stories to encourage others to come to Jesus simply
to touch his cloak.

Reflection

Spend some time in silence and think about your journey
of faith, the history of your coming to Jesus. Recall the
people in your lifetime who shared their faith stories. Who
pointed you to Jesus? Give thanks for their courage to share
their stories. Thank God for using these testimonies as
instruments of grace in your life.

Focus for today

Listen carefully to how people talk about God. Thank God
for words of affirmation and encouragement. When people
use God's name in vain, take the opportunity to share graciously with them what this God has done for you.

Prayer

We thank you, Almighty God, that you bring people across
our paths who share their faith journey openly and freely.
We thank you for the miracles that these testimonies lead
to. During the course of this day, may we listen carefully
to the Spirit's prompting to point people toward Jesus so
that they too may touch his cloak and experience healing.
Amen.

DAY 12 † TUESDAY

Jesus, who fulfills needs

🕮 Read Mark 6:35-44

*E*NOUGH IS NEVER enough, is it? We want to earn more, drive better cars, live in bigger houses. We are never satisfied with our bodies. We desire more and better. Our lives do not seem worth living with the material goods we have and the bodies we occupy. "There simply isn't enough. Can't you see that, Jesus?"

In the disciples' minds and ours as well, the fish and the loaves appear insufficient to meet the needs in their midst. But then Jesus surprises his disciples by taking what they have and making it enough. We acknowledge this truth every time we pray the Lord's Prayer: "Give us this day our daily bread."

When we pray this line of the Lord's Prayer, do we pray it sincerely? It speaks of God's ability to give us enough to keep going. God takes what we have already, despite its seeming insufficiency, and transforms it into sustenance that energizes us and blesses those around us.

"But Lord, I don't have enough patience to face this day!" Well, we give God what we have and see what happens. It may surprise us to see how many people God will feed in this day through our exercise of tolerance and self-control. God does not expect us to come fully equipped for every scenario. God is the One who can take little and create abundance. We may find it tempting at this point to offer God our bank balances, expecting exponential growth overnight. Remember what the Lord's Prayer suggests: God gives enough to meet our needs. When we start appreciating God's providence in this manner, we will soon find that there is more than enough left over to continue being a blessing to others.

Reflection

How much of your life is driven by a consumerist attitude? How content are you with what you have? How often do you feel that your life is insufficient when you don't have a particular item? Well, look around you. Look inside yourself. What do you have already? Hand this to God, and allow God to do the rest.

Focus for today

Be aware of those in your community who do not share the same luxuries that you have taken for granted. Select one item that you would cling to with all your life—like a hungry disciple clutching to the fish and bread in the midst of a hungry crowd—and hand it to Jesus. Ask how you can use this one possession to bless those around you.

Prayer

Jesus, miraculously you can take the little we have and transform it into bread and drink to soothe the hungry and quench the thirst of those in need. Take what we have; but we pray, give us today our daily bread. Amen.

DAY 13 † WEDNESDAY

Jesus, who calms the storms

🌿 Read Mark 6:48-51*a*

*T*HIS FAMILIAR STORY calls to mind Jesus' inviting Peter to step out onto the water. Mark does not mention Peter at all in this account, whereas Matthew focuses on Peter's determination to emulate Jesus by doing the seemingly impossible. Mark draws our attention to a different aspect of the story. Mark focuses not on Jesus' ability to walk on water but on his creating peace. It is as if the disciples' fear and the storm intertwine. Jesus' offer of peace and the subsiding of the storm are linked. "'Take heart, it is I; do not be afraid.' Then he got into the boat with them and the wind ceased."

I imagine we can all tell stories of how Jesus climbed into our boat and brought peace. Many of us could testify to the calming of storms once we acknowledged Jesus' presence with us.

What we find even more astonishing is the way that Jesus often comes to us! We naturally expect God to appear in a flash of light, in writing on the wall, or through some other supernatural event. We may even decide that it would be impossible for God to get to where we are, rocking and swaying in the middle of stormy water. But Jesus often surprises us, walking on these tumultuous waters as if they were no threat to him at all!

The disciples are afraid. Naturally they fear drowning, but their fear only increases as an unknown shape walks toward them on the water. Then Jesus comes into their place of fear and calls them to peace. He steps into the boat, and the wind dies down. We too can know the peace of Jesus in any situation that generates fear and regret.

Reflection

Jesus can come straight through your place of fear and desperation. Recall a time when God came to you in the most unexpected way.

Focus for today

Remind those around you that Jesus can come to them in the midst of their turmoil and fear. Facing threats with Jesus in the boat makes circumstances manageable.

Prayer

Creating and calming God, the winds die down when we invite you to share our time and space. We acknowledge, Lord, that our problems do not magically disappear when you climb into our boats, but you remind us that nothing we face is more powerful than you. Today we face our challenges knowing that we are not alone but embraced by your peace, which is beyond our understanding. Amen.

DAY 14 † THURSDAY

Jesus, who saves the "others"

🐚 Read Mark 7:24-30

I HAVE GROWN extremely wary of faith healers. They tend to drift in and out of towns, advertising that God will perform miracles on such and such a day at such and such a place. I attended one of these rallies once and was shocked to hear the preacher telling people that if they had enough faith, God would be persuaded to heal them. Simply spoken, if no miracle took place, it reflected on the person's faith. Among those in attendance at these rallies are those who have faith and receive healing and "the others" who do not qualify for healing for whatever reason.

To devout Jews, the Syrophoenician woman falls into the latter category because she is not a Jew. By telling this story, the Gospel writer Mark is breaking new ground. This woman possibly represents Gentile converts among the early Jesus followers. Through many different stories, Mark portrays a Jesus who came to save the house of Israel first—but not the house of Israel only. Jesus' love stretches beyond culture, borders, philosophies, and even religion! Jesus touches this woman's life (and that of her daughter) despite the fact that she is not Jewish.

God's love breaks through human barriers and definitions so all can know and experience God's presence. What barrier do you struggle with? Is it racism, even in its subtlest forms? Do you view the poor in a different way from your own reflection in the mirror? Whose life do you believe is beyond God's reach? Perhaps we erect barriers related to our intolerance of people of different faiths. Read through this passage again and envision the person you just imagined in the place of the woman. Jesus can touch our lives and the lives of "the others."

Reflection

You may have been hurt by people who are different from you. It may be difficult to forgive them, let alone acknowledge that God cares as much about them as about you. Perhaps your hesitancy toward certain groups of people is part of your family history. How can God convince you that these folks are your brothers and sisters in Christ?

Focus for today

Whenever you feel tempted to stereotype people as inferior, pray that God will open your eyes to their humanity and to God's acts of love in their lives.

Prayer

Jesus our Lord, how we deprive ourselves of your kingdom vision when we deny others the possibility of serving a God who is righteous and just. Heal us, O Lord. Amen.

DAY 15 † FRIDAY

Jesus, who draws us aside

🐚 Read Mark 7:31-37

I WONDER WHAT this man thinks when Jesus takes him aside? What goes through his mind as Jesus puts his fingers in his ears, spits, and touches his tongue? This is certainly one of Jesus' strangest approaches toward one who comes for healing. On many other occasions, Jesus only said a few words or simply touched—and a healing miracle occurred.

We don't know the man's expectations, but Jesus manages to surprise us with this elaborate act of healing. The phrase that catches my eye is this: "He took him aside in private." Many other miracles took place in public, but this passage implies that Jesus ministers to this man out of public view. In this setting, Jesus' actions and words appear more personalized. This is no generic miracle. It is meant for this man and for him only. Jesus touches the man's ear and tongue, the parts most apparent as needing healing.

I began thinking, *If Jesus drew me aside, which areas of my life would he touch?* I have come to know that in my busyness, I can hide the broken areas of my life. But when I spend time alone with God, God cuts through the clutter of my life, points out and touches the parts that require the divine touch. I may feel more comfortable listening to Jesus in the midst of the crowds, to see Jesus touch the lives of others. But when Jesus and I meet "in private," he directs his words to me and his touch comes my way. Jesus continues to draw me aside from time to time—away from my schedule, from other people, and possibly my pride.

For what reason does Jesus draw you aside? What areas of your life need that healing touch?

Reflection

How busy is your life? How much time do you spend among people? When did you last spend quality time alone with God?

Focus for today

God's time with you is not generic. The Holy One knows your needs and your shortcomings. Dare to become vulnerable in the divine presence, and allow God to touch your life.

Prayer

O God, you know the healing we need as communities and as individuals. I am grateful to be counted as one of your unique children. Draw me aside, Lord, and touch my life where I need your healing the most. Amen.

DAY 16 † SATURDAY

What comprises your "daily bread"?

How does your faith change when Jesus approaches you on stormy waters?

What do you feel when Jesus touches the lives of those you cannot view as your equals?

When Jesus draws you aside, which part of your life does he focus on?

DAY 17 † MONDAY

Jesus, who uses the ordinary

🕊 Read Mark 8:1-9

$\mathcal{A}$ SECOND TIME Mark tells the story of Jesus feeding a crowd with loaves and fish. This account strongly resembles the first. A large crowd follows Jesus. The people find themselves far from the markets and cannot purchase food. The disciples bring Jesus some loaves and a few fish, and he feeds the multitude with what they offer. After everyone eats, there is food left over. Why does Mark repeat the story? Perhaps Mark wants to get a point across: what we have is enough for Jesus.

We sometimes fail to respond to God's call on our lives because we feel inadequate to the task—as if what we have to offer God will not suffice. I often hear stories of people's call to ministry, of people believing that God wants them to be instruments of hope and love to others. Many list all sorts of reasons for their unworthiness of such a calling: not smart enough, inadequate experience, or no trust of people. They don't feel they have what it takes. Today's scripture passage stresses that Jesus can take what we have and make it enough.

We may walk this Lenten road with excuses in our heart, reasons God cannot use us. Our self-inflicted reasons try to counter God's power of transformation. Let us step out in faith and take the risk. Hungry multitudes await, and what we offer will be enough to reveal God's love in God's power and grace.

Reflection

You may believe that parts of your life aren't good enough for God. While meaningful to you, many parts of your life seem to be of little benefit to others. Name these. Say to God, "I don't have much. This is it. Lord, it is up to you. Use me as you see fit."

Focus for today

Empower those around you by recognizing the small aspects of their lives that they think are of no use to anyone. Point them out, and describe how these particular qualities have enriched your life without their knowing.

Prayer

Why, Lord, do we keep trying to convince ourselves that we are not good enough for you? We think that by going to church religiously, by reading our Bibles repeatedly, we somehow prove ourselves worthy. May we realize that these activities reside over and above what you see in us. Take who we are, and help us feed those who hunger. Amen.

DAY 18 † TUESDAY

Jesus, who heals continuously

🕊 Read Mark 8:22-26

𝒯HE QUESTION BECKONS: Why didn't Jesus heal this man perfectly the first time? Compared to other miracles, this one does not seem to require more of Jesus' power or effort. So why the second intervention? Some may argue that the man's lack of faith invalidated the first attempt—an argument that clutches at straws. Our question looks for someone to blame for the delay in this man's restoration.

We hear similar views expressed as people attempt to make sense of a lack of healing: "Your sins stand in the way of God touching your life," or "You won't be healed because you have not forgiven," or "God will only heal you when you have reached rock bottom." This account offers a rich lesson: healing is a process. When we pray for God's intervention in our lives, it does not always happen in the blink of an eye. At times, God guides us slowly, step-by-step, toward places of healing.

Take, for instance, the ability to forgive. We may decide to forgive and pray for God's involvement in the process, but we still feel awkward spending time with the recipients of our forgiveness. Yet, the more we pray and the more we engage these people, the less apt we are to allow anger, resentment, and bad feelings to blind us. After a while we may start seeing silhouettes of the people behind the events and come to a moment when we can look people in the eyes again without the coloration of our own hurts.

We might ponder God's continuous touch in our lives before the healing comes. We can think back to the different stages of healing that we have experienced and recognize God's repeated prodding, leading, and questioning. Eventually we arrived where God wanted us to be.

Reflection

We base much of our existence on the notion of instant gratification. That notion even drives our economies. How much of your walk with God is directed by your desire for God's instantaneous intervention? How does the word *process* feature in your spirituality?

Focus for today

Be aware of processes that exist all around you: the caterpillar turning into a butterfly, children growing and developing new abilities daily. God is not finished with you yet. Embrace the process of being and becoming and the way God touches your life again and again.

Prayer

God of second touches, there is no touch like yours. Blind and seeking sight, we succumb to the instant desires of our hearts and demand that you, O God, grant these desires within our time frames. Help us to wait, to see, to feel, and to know that you remain in control. Amen.

DAY 19 † WEDNESDAY

Jesus, who gives faith

🕊 Read Mark 9:14-29

*T*O ME, VERSE 24 ("'I believe; help my unbelief!'") stands out as a fitting prayer for Lent. When John Wesley reflected on this verse, he explained it in the following words: "Although my faith be so small, that it might rather be termed unbelief, yet help me."[2] At no moment in our lives do we have sufficient faith. The very nature of our journey with God entails our desire to believe more.

We may deem our current state of faith as lacking in comparison to life's challenges. Do we exhibit enough faith and belief in God to make it through this day? We may answer yes reluctantly. What about having enough faith and belief in God to make it through the next week, the next month, the next year, or even the next decade?

Thankfully, God asks us to believe enough only for the "now," the present, the moment. When life's surprises stretch our faith in God, then we—with the boy's father— can pray, "'I believe; help my unbelief!'"

I wonder how the father would have described his belief *after* his son's healing. Does he find himself awe-struck that Jesus can bring about this healing despite his lack of confidence in his own faith? Does he leave that place feeling that anything is possible with Jesus? Perhaps he leaves trusting God again after his initial disillusion-ment with the disciples' inability to help.

Picture the end of this story. In my mind's eye, I see a young man walking home, freed from evil spirits. I imag-ine a father and a son, arms around each other's shoulder, talking with great joy and celebrating what has taken place . . . despite the father's sense of unbelief.

Reflection

How many times have you heard Christians say that God failed to act due to someone's lack of faith? What does today's passage teach you about God's providence?

Focus for today

When life's challenges confront you today and you feel unable to cope, pray the father's prayer: "I believe; help my unbelief!" Let God demonstrate divine compassion at work even when your faith and belief in God seem insufficient.

Prayer

Almighty God, we believe. Help our unbelief. Thank you for not measuring our faith before acting in our lives. Your actions help us believe more in who you are and what you can do. In Jesus' name. Amen.

DAY 20 † THURSDAY

Jesus, who hears the lowly

🕊 Read Mark 10:46-52

🕊

"WHAT DO YOU WANT ME to do for you?" Jesus had asked the same question of the sons of Zebedee. (See Mark 10:36.) In the preceding passage (Mark 10:32-45) Jesus had just rebuked these men for their selfish request to sit on his right and his left at the time when he takes power. James and John may have felt a bit disgruntled. They have walked with Jesus, listened to Jesus, and followed all his commands. They think that must count for something. *Why won't Jesus grant this one request as a token of gratitude for their faithfulness?*

In today's passage, we read the story of Bartimaeus. Surely Bartimaeus does not waken that morning expecting to be sighted later the same day. He certainly does not think, *By this time tomorrow the greatest challenge of my life will be resolved.* He sits at the city gates as he has done all the mornings before. He hears that Jesus will pass by, but he has no appointment to see him. He has no status, title, or position that will draw Jesus' attention. All he can do is cry out, "Jesus, Son of David, have mercy on me!"

Jesus hears his cry, stops, and calls for Bartimaeus. He then restores Bartimaeus's sight. Jesus' interaction with Bartimaeus differs greatly from his interaction with James and John. Jesus rebukes arrogant assumptions that imply God owes us something, but he gives generously to the man who can only shout from the gutters for a bit of God's attention. Surely, as this man follows Jesus into Jerusalem, he cannot take his eyes off Jesus, celebrating the one who gave him back his sight.

How do you approach this Lenten time of surrender and healing? Perhaps we think that we deserve recognition for being spiritually strong because of our commitment to this journey. Jesus' response may surprise us, "No, I don't owe you anything." Instead, dare to be truthful with yourself. Seek healing for the real diseases in your life. Take a step back, and cry out to Jesus from the gutters. He will hear your voice, call for you, and respond in a fitting way.

Reflection

In what ways have you assumed that God owes you? When have you negotiated with God, saying, "Lord, I have been a faithful servant. I think it is time that you . . . "?

Focus for today

Refrain from using faithfulness as a bargaining tool to convince God to do your will. Know that God meets you, even in the gutters.

Prayer

Help me when I am at the end of my wisdom and effort, O Lord. May I never use my devotion to you as currency to negotiate your involvement in my life. Amen.

DAY 21 † FRIDAY

Jesus, who seeks fruit

🕊 Read Mark 11:12-25

THE GOSPEL WRITER cleverly splits in two the story of the curse of the fig tree, interjecting Jesus' address to the money changers and merchants in the Temple. Perhaps Mark links these two events in his mind. Certainly the two events contain some parallels: Jesus goes to the fig tree to see if it has any fruit but finds none. Jesus goes to the Temple, maybe to worship, but finds nothing but bartering, negotiating, and greed. Jesus proclaims that no one shall eat from the tree again and observes that the Temple has been made "a den of robbers." Jesus' expectation of fruit out of season seems a bit unfair, but I think Mark used the tree as a prop to illustrate another point altogether. Trees have seasons for fruit bearing, but it is always fruit-bearing season for the people of God.

When viewing our faith, our churches, or our ministries, God hopes to see devoted lives rather than bickering, negotiating the value of another's faith, or measuring the worth of others' commitment to God. If we reduce our spirituality to pride and infighting, then Jesus' words are damning but true: "May no one ever eat fruit from you again."

We need to keep before us and our worshiping communities the purpose of the Christian life. It is not about making the most money or occupying the fanciest church buildings. It is not about the many mission projects or home groups that we boast about, comparing our brand of Christianity to the church next door. The Christian life and the life of worship involve the gift of presence. This presence in our communities requires us to be the people and places where folk can feel connected with God and in fellowship with other Christ-followers. This approach requires us to deny ourselves and to live in the belief that Christ is indeed the Lord of his church. If Jesus came to you today, would he meet a Christ-follower?

Reflection

What defines your life? In the order of influence, what aspects of your life dictate who you are? Are you first a businessperson, then a sportsperson, and then a Christian? In what area does Christ need to be first so that your entire being bears evidence of his lordship?

Focus for today

Challenge yourself and other Christ-followers to put God first. When you walk into your place of worship, what is the first message you give through your words and actions? Pursue an action that conveys God's love.

Prayer

Compassionate and caring God, you are quick to forgive and eager to restore. We know that at times we use our faith and our places of worship as instruments to advance our own agendas. We do this to soothe our own consciences, hoping to prove ourselves worthy of your love. Help us bear fruit, the fruit of the Spirit, so that others may come, eat, and be satisfied. Amen.

DAY 22 † SATURDAY

When have you felt that you had insufficient faith? How did God respond?

"What do you want me to do for you?" Jesus asks. How do you answer this question?

If Jesus looked for fruit in your life, what would he find?

What fruit is evident in your faith community?

THE GOSPEL OF MATTHEW

Getting to Know Jesus in Our Faith

MATTHEW WROTE HIS ACCOUNT to a Jewish audience, people who thought they already knew God. While Mark introduces Jesus as "someone new," Matthew speaks about Jesus as the one the Israelites should already know. For some, Christianity is an inherited religion. Allow Matthew to bring this person of Christ to life, coming to know Jesus as more than a character in the faith to which we adhere.

DAY 23 † MONDAY

Jesus, who moves beyond religious form

🕊 Read Matthew 8:5-13

$\mathcal{A}$ SET STRUCTURE GUIDES the centurion's world—the military way. For him, everything functions within this worldview. Military framework shapes his identity and influences the way he interacts with others. Soldiers address their superiors in particular ways in military life. Here we see the centurion applying this structure to the way he approaches Jesus. He prepares to meet Jesus using his *own* frame of reference, his *own* language, and in a manner appropriate to greeting a superior in the Roman army.

The centurion does not set his worldview aside or change his language in order to fit into a Jewish mold. He comes to Jesus as he is, for that is the best he knows—and Jesus receives him in that way. Jesus even speaks to him in a language he understands, instructing him: "Go; let it be done for you according to your faith." How strange that we tend to "leave our lives at the door" when we prepare to meet with Jesus! We may consider our lives too unacceptable or believe that Jesus would not receive us as we are. So we change the way we speak or change the way we conduct ourselves when we meet with Jesus. It's a pity that we forget that Jesus meets us everywhere and speaks our language.

This scripture recounts the potential of allowing Jesus to speak the language of the workplace. Jesus knows the customs and habits of our family lives. We might be surprised when we take the risk of saying to Jesus, "You are not boxed in at a certain place; speak to us in ways that are familiar to us at work or at home."

Besides the miraculous healing of the servant, another miracle takes place in this story: a person experiences the work of God in a language and manner that occurs outside the confines of human religious structures. Churches and places of worship *are* special, but we make a mistake in thinking that God resides and acts only there—totally removed from our daily activities.

Reflection

Put yourself in the centurion's shoes. A work colleague may desire God's work in his or her life. Using familiar language and structures, speak to Jesus about the matter. What would your conversation sound like? Allow Jesus to encounter you in this way.

Focus for today

At work or at home, be in continuous prayer using words or expressions common to that context.

Prayer

Dear Lord, speak to me today at work and at home. I pray that I will find healing from thinking that you are located only at church or in the worshiping community. You know my context at work and at home. Remind me constantly that you are there. Amen.

DAY 24 † TUESDAY

Jesus, who knows better

🕊 Read Matthew 9:27-31

*T*HESE MEN MUST HAVE HEARD of Jesus' presence and the miracles he has performed. Perhaps someone led them to Jesus. They will not remain silent, knowing that Jesus is near. They call Jesus by the title "Son of David," a title reserved for the Messiah who would come to heal and deliver God's people. We can sense their great excitement when they hear Jesus ask, "Do you believe that I am able to do this?"

It is one thing to cry to God for help; it is another to surrender to God, trusting that God can and will intervene. Have you ever undergone surgery? Can you recall family discussions about how a certain procedure would rectify a problem? Did you, when you rolled into surgery and the anesthetist prepared to administer the anesthesia, raise questions about the surgeon's competence, about whether the surgeon had the correct file with the right procedure, and whether the procedure would really solve the problem? Well, at this point you have to let go and trust the person in charge.

Have we been praying for an intervention, an act of God in our lives? How do we respond to Jesus' question, "Do you believe that I am able to do this?" We may be tempted to respond, "Yes, Lord, as long as you do it in this way or that way. As long as you manage it within this time frame or in that place." Surrendering to God demands more than trust that God can act. It demands the trust that God has the knowledge and wisdom to know how to act, when to act, and where to act. Today's reading encourages us to pray for healing of a different kind: a healing from only partial trust in God's ability to work in our lives. Believe that God has heard you. Surrender all; place yourself in God's grace, for God knows best.

Reflection

Consider the issues and problems that you have been bringing to God in prayer. Offer these to God, one by one. Hear God ask you each time, "Do you believe that I am able to do this?" Respond to God in prayer.

Focus for today

As you proceed through this day, pray that God will open your eyes to God's involvement in your life. God's hand at work may be escaping your notice. Give thanks for these times and places of divine intervention.

Prayer

Son of David, have mercy on us. May we see your grace and love at work in our lives. We surrender all to you, trusting in your infinite ability, understanding, and love. Amen.

DAY 25 † WEDNESDAY

Jesus, who challenges our explanations

🕊 Read Matthew 9:32-33

NOTICE THE DIVERSE RESPONSES to this miracle. The crowd is amazed. "Never has anything like this been seen in Israel." The Pharisees believe that Jesus knows too much about demons and deduce that his power derives from an evil source. In the midst of the ecstasy and condemnation stands a healed man! Does he care whether an event like this has ever been witnessed in all of Israel? Will he entertain a debate about whether his newfound freedom results from demonic activity?

To this man, Jesus is the source of this special gift in his life. The Pharisees never offered him healing. The crowd only gave him pity or an occasional gift. Jesus sets him free from the constraints of being unable to express himself. It would not have mattered to him what the crowd or the Pharisees said. His testimony will focus on Jesus who defied expectations, drove out the demon, and healed him!

Where do we stand when God acts in our lives? The God-event may so impress us that we forget to celebrate with other people. Sometimes we might write off God's handiwork through the constructs of our thinking. This miracle goes beyond the healing of a mute demoniac. This healing bears testimony to how God works and who God chooses as instruments of God's self-revelation.

Jesus' healing of a mute demoniac demonstrates the superiority of God's power. This man's healing opens the eyes of the crowd to witness what they have never seen before. The healing of this unlikely person places the religious authorities in a position of questioning what they believe about healing and where they believe healing comes from. May God challenge our perspectives about how God can act in our lives.

Reflection

Think about the unusual ways God has reached out to you. When has God used your weaknesses to speak to others about God's amazing power of love and healing?

Focus for today

Be mindful of God's voice speaking through the "mute demoniacs" that you encounter. Listen carefully; watch closely, because you may see something that has never been witnessed before!

Prayer

Open my eyes, God, so that I may see your hand at work in my life today. Thank you for using the most unlikely people, the most inappropriate events, to speak the truth of your love. In Jesus' name. Amen.

DAY 26 † THURSDAY

Jesus, who shows tolerance

🕊 Read Matthew 17:24-27

*M*Y WIFE BOUGHT ME a mug with the following inscription: "I may not always be right, but I am never wrong!" How true that is of my life. I know that at times I hold to my perspective with all my might, especially when I am convinced that the other party is wrong. You see, I am never wrong! (I say this in jest!)

In this passage we read that although Jesus pays the Temple tax, he does so reluctantly. He does not fully support the measure, but he abides by the current understanding. He could have stood his ground and said, "No, because I don't think it's right." Not Jesus! He performs a miracle—not to show that he knows better or to amaze his friends with his ability to produce money from a fish's mouth. Jesus offers the following reason: "So that we do not give offense to them" [the collectors of the Temple tax].

Does Jesus compromise his own position? No; Jesus realizes that it takes nothing away from him to pay these taxes, even if he knows better. Jesus respects these people, their views, and the practice of giving tax to the Temple.

Jesus' action challenges us. We fill our days with the quest of winning the argument by proving that we are right and showing up the incorrectness of others' beliefs, practices, or choices. Suppose we attempt to go through a day holding on to our truth but giving others the respect of holding on to theirs? Sometimes we must stand up for what we believe is right, but we choose those moments carefully and add a dollop of grace. To walk the way of peace requires that we lead lives of tolerance, trying to understand and respect views that differ from our own. We don't have to be right all the time, and we aren't.

Reflection

Do you feel the need to express your views no matter what? How often will you stand your ground to prove a point? Think about your persistence in being right, either at home or at work. How much value does this add to your relationships, and how does it facilitate other people's ability to express their thoughts to you freely?

Focus for today

Before jumping on your soapbox, take some time to ponder Jesus' response to this situation. Create the possibility of compromise when different opinions come to the fore.

Prayer

Prince of Peace, you managed to respect the views of those who opposed you without surrendering your own truth. We can learn a lot from you in this regard. Fill us with wisdom, discernment, and the ability to seek the way of peace and not to cause offense. Amen.

THE GOSPEL OF LUKE

Getting to Know Jesus of the Marginalized

THIS ACCOUNT OF THE JESUS story focuses on those who are in pain, both physically and emotionally. Luke focuses on the marginalized, those who would not be considered worthy of God's approach. Luke speaks more about women, foreigners, and the poor than any other Gospel writer. He invites those who sit on the edges of the crowd to hear the good news of God's love. He addresses his account in the form of a letter. Receive these miracles as a letter of love and encouragement to you.

DAY 27 † FRIDAY

Jesus, who challenges our certainties

🕊 Read Luke 5:4-11

W<small>E</small> ALL HAVE OUR FIELDS of expertise that center on our gifts, abilities, learned skills, or occupations. Several of the disciples knew how to fish. They grew up on the boats. Their fathers and grandfathers probably made a living this way. If we wanted to know anything about catching fish, we would be well served to spend time with Jesus' closest companions.

Thinking about fields of expertise, we may know how it feels to have someone looking over our shoulder and telling us we should be doing things differently. We don't take kindly to this instruction and probably find it even more frustrating when we don't know much about the persons making the comments.

So we commend Simon for his response to Jesus. It must have taken great humility and a bucketful of faith to say, "If you say so, I will . . . " I don't believe Simon complies, thinking, *I'll do it, but you'll see that it won't work.* There is something genuine and sincere about his compliance. Besides the miracle of abundant fish, we witness a miracle taking place in Simon's character. In the Gospels, we come to know Simon as a fiery personality, someone who liked following his own mind. Here we view him as a man of faith in a moment of humility.

Today we will focus on letting go of our I-know-it-all attitudes. In moments where all seems in vain or in moments where we simply do not know where to turn, we can quiet ourselves, turn to God, and find a place where we can say to God, "If you say so, I will . . . ," even when God speaks through a colleague, spouse, child, or friend. We will stand in awe of the miracles of abundance that our humility and faith allow God to bring to pass.

Reflection

Recall a time when, although you were at a loss, you insisted on doing things your own way. How would things have worked out if you had put your pride in your pocket and listened to someone else's advice?

Focus for today

Listen more and speak less. Give those around you the opportunity to share their ideas, and make a concerted effort to include in conversation those who do not usually share their views. God may provide wisdom through the least expected vessel.

Prayer

You know it all, Lord. We don't. Our self-confidence pushes us to the edge, and we drive others and you away. Challenge us and move us to be more humble and to trust in your guidance. Amen.

DAY 28 † SATURDAY

In what areas have you grown this past week?

What language has God used to reach out to you?

"Do you believe that I am able to do this?" Describe God's involvement in your life since God asked you this question.

Jesus breaks through our boundaries; he acts despite the self-imposed confines of our philosophies or beliefs. Describe one belief Jesus has challenged during this past week.

DAY 29 † MONDAY

Jesus, who restores hope

🕊 Read Luke 7:11-15

WIDOWS HAD IT TOUGH during Jesus' day. Unlike the modern era, women commonly did not have occupations that brought in money. No insurance policies, pensions, or government grants helped widows survive financially. They gleaned the fields for food or went to the Temple for assistance. When the father of a household died, his brother usually took the responsibility to look after his wife. When there was a son in the family, he would take care of his mother. This passage tells us of a widow who has lost her only son. Not only must she contend with losing her child, but she faces the terrifying prospect of survival without a breadwinner in the house.

We read that Jesus notices what is taking place before his eyes and feels compassion for her. The miracle of raising the widow's son has value just as it is. But Jesus addresses more than a mother's grief for her departed child. By raising her son, he also restores her dignity. This widow will have her son back; he may be the only family she has. She will not be alone. Furthermore, she will not have to beg for food or depend on the gifts of others.

Jesus restores the young man to life and his mother to dignity and joy. With a few words, Jesus changes her present and her future. She and her son will awaken every morning knowing that God provides.

This passage calls us to awareness of our ability to serve as instruments of hope and dignity to those we pass in the streets. Take some lessons from Jesus today. Look around, notice people, and attempt to understand their situations. The time of Lent beckons us to look beyond self and to become God's hands at work in the lives of people all around us.

Reflection

Jesus and his disciples could have walked past the funeral procession that day. Instead, Jesus stopped, looked, and felt. What prevents you from stopping, looking, and feeling?

Focus for today

Focus on an action that will bring dignity to a person forgotten by family, the church, or even society. You could do something seemingly insignificant; simply listening might enable that person to feel a sense of self-worth.

Prayer

Almighty God, we so easily walk past the suffering and pain of people around us. Even when we think we know their pain, we do not take note of their deeper struggles. Help me today to follow your example—to stop, to look, to feel compassion, and to engage. Amen.

DAY 30 † TUESDAY

Jesus, who works unlikely miracles

Read Luke 11:14-17

SOME IN THE CROWD missed the point. They neglected to celebrate the miracle that took place in their midst and chose to argue about the way Jesus managed to perform these amazing wonders. How is it possible that people can reject the work of God out-of-hand because it seems impossible that this should actually be taking place at all?

But let us not be too hasty in pointing fingers at members of the crowd, for what they were doing takes place in the household of God with uncomfortable regularity. Take, for instance, arguments that occur in church around something as "sacred" as the furnishings in the church, the way hymns are sung, what musical instruments are permitted in worship services, even how long the preacher should be preaching. All these grumblings take place while we miss the miracle of sins forgiven, a connection between a person and God during a hymn, or the kneeling at the altar of the most unlikely people to share in any meal, let alone the meal of the Lord's Supper.

The healing of the mute demoniac is over in the blink of an eye. It takes only one verse to describe this miracle. The healed person fades into the background as the conversation about the legitimacy of the miracle takes over. The passionate voices of those who thought they were right grow louder and louder as the restored voice of the healed demoniac whispers away. Their arguing mutes his voice once again. So does ours.

How about rethinking our attitudes toward the work of God taking place in our midst? Of course we will find every possible reason to debate and argue the mechanics of lives that change, but we will never be able to capture that moment within our own power when a person stands up and says, "I have been released!" Celebrate Jesus today. Rejoice that Jesus can perform the miracles which we may not think to be appropriate for God.

Reflection

Has anybody argued the fact that your life has been changed by God? Did the person find the occasion too good to be true? Pray that your eyes will be open to the possibility of God at work in people whom you least expect to be recipients of God's grace.

Focus for today

Find every reason to celebrate the work of God today. Celebrate how God changes lives, heals attitudes, and restores relationships. When others argue about petty things in the life of the faith community, draw their attention to the possibility of God at work in the midst of that which causes their strife.

Prayer

God of unexplained miracles, we confess today that we are people of conflict. We find reasons for conflict even when miracles take place before our eyes. We even dare to argue about the legitimacy of your work. Forgive us, O God, and help us to celebrate all that you do. Amen.

DAY 31 † WEDNESDAY

Jesus, who offers renewed perspective

🐚 Read Luke 13:10-17

*M*Y CLERGY COLLEAGUES and I often talk together about the text on which we are going to preach the following Sunday. When we discussed this passage, my friend Themba mentioned that he had heard a sermon on the passage titled "All she could see was dust." This phrase milled through my mind for the rest of the week, and I could picture the story unfolding in front of my eyes. As it did, I thought that this miracle actually could be called the miracle of renewed perspective. Imagine Jesus teaching in the synagogue. Jesus looks through the open door and sees a woman who is bent over. He calls her in, speaks to her, touches her, and heals her.

When have life's worries weighed you down so much that all you see is the ground beneath you? In what situations have you simply survived by placing one foot in front of another, slowly moving forward? Perhaps you need a Jesus-touch to help you stand up straight and look at the world from a new perspective.

Other perspectives may have changed that day as well. The leader of the synagogue and the onlookers probably don't take much notice of this woman at first. Maybe they see her as just another person with unfortunate struggles. We too see people, but we don't take note of their pain. Encountering their struggles, we may feel inadequate because we don't know how to assist. Like the synagogue leader we have turned from those in need, using the excuse that it is not the right time or the right place for them to receive assistance.

But Jesus takes note. Jesus speaks and touches. The woman went into the synagogue bent over and walked out upright. The leader may have walked into the synagogue quite confident but left a bit humbled, perhaps with head bent down as he realized his own insensitivity. All this occurs because Jesus speaks. When Jesus speaks into your life today, how will your perspective change?

Reflection

Think about your struggles. What occupies your attention? Can you see only the small piece of ground beneath your feet? Can you see the needs of others? Do you see people but not their pain?

Focus for today

Pray that you may meet Jesus, hear Jesus, and feel Jesus in the midst of your struggles. Trust that when you encounter God, your perspective will change. Be sensitive to the needs of others, for you may be their answer to prayer.

Prayer

Gracious God, when you speak we see things differently. Your voice brings new possibilities and for this we thank you. We pray that as we journey with you and you with us, we will find healing. May our eyes be open to those around us and may we, like you, find time to call them in, speak to them, touch them with your love and compassion. In Jesus' name. Amen.

DAY 32 † THURSDAY

Jesus, who notices and acts

🍃 Read Luke 14:1-4

DROPSY IS A CONDITION where liquid accumulates and is retained in the body due to an illness of the heart, liver, kidneys, or brain. It often displays itself through the excessive swelling of the abdomen or the limbs.

It is the sabbath and Jesus is on his way to share in a meal with a leader of the Pharisees. As he walks, Jesus notices a man with dropsy. This man must have attracted some attention, looking different from those who passed him by. Jesus turns and asks the lawyers and Pharisees who accompany him whether it is lawful to heal on the sabbath. Their silence in response to this provocative question speaks volumes. They must have noticed this man, but what could they do? And even if they could heal him, it was the sabbath! Strictly speaking, healing amounted to work, and work was forbidden on the sabbath.

The lawyers and Pharisees find themselves caught between a rock and a hard place. Jesus proceeds nevertheless and touches this man's life. He notices and acts, unlike the other people who simply notice and fail to act, perhaps believing that they cannot make a difference.

This miracle offers a lesson about God's willingness to intervene. Can we picture Jesus walking with us, and when we notice persons' needs but fail to act, asking us whether it is ok; is it the right time to touch, to act, to intervene? Instead of silence, we may sincerely offer God the following reasons for our inaction: "Lord, they are that way because they are lazy"; "Lord, it won't help to get involved there, because they won't appreciate it"; "Lord, did you consider their past behavior? If I were you, I'd leave them that way."

Jesus posed the question, not to seek permission to intervene, but to draw from those around him their understanding of grace (or lack thereof). Jesus touched the man's life with grace that day, because Jesus noticed and acted. Perhaps his action challenges the lawyers and Pharisees. It is not enough to notice. It is imperative to act, even when our social structures suggest that it may not be the right time or the right place to do so.

Reflection

To whom do you offer only a courtesy glance, without acknowledging the possibility of God's hand at work in their lives? Of whom is God speaking when God turns to you and asks: "Is it ok for me to touch them today?"

Focus for today

Be particularly aware of people who share your space. Be sensitive to those who display a need, and attempt to reach out to them.

Prayer

How uncomfortable it is when you ask those difficult questions, O God—when you force us to look beyond ourselves and see those around us. We no longer notice the presence of the suffering in our churches or in our neighborhoods. Perhaps we do, but we would rather ignore it. Open our eyes, Lord. In Jesus' name. Amen.

DAY 33 † FRIDAY

Jesus, who works when we forget

✤ Read Luke 17:11-19

*M*Y BIBLE STUDY GROUP was discussing this passage, and I recall someone saying, "Those ungrateful people! If I were Jesus, I would give their leprosy back!" Judgment comes easily with this passage. Read verses 14 and 15 again. We might reflect that these men will receive healing only when they show themselves to the priests. Maybe they think so too. But one man realizes that he has been healed while on the way, and he turns back.

I can identify with those who neglect to thank Jesus for a miracle performed. I acknowledge my total absorption in praying to God about a particular issue. At that time I could fathom nothing else in the world but my problem. As I journeyed further, healing came slowly; I eventually found myself in a place of healing while forgetting that I had prayed in earnest for God's intervention. It is a bit like the joke of a person driving into a parking lot, praying, *Lord, please help me find a parking spot close to the entrance.* While praying, the person spots a vacant space in front of the door and quickly adds to the prayer, *Don't worry, Lord; I found one!*

How wonderful it would be if we actually took the time to recognize God's hand at work in our lives. Those who keep prayer journals often testify to the fact that prayers long forgotten receive answers in the most amazing ways. Perhaps the time has come to turn from our busy wanderings and to thank God for miracles and healing that occur while on the way.

Reflection

God is at work behind the scenes in ways that you cannot direct or comprehend. Share a story with someone of how God has answered a prayer in your life, a prayer that you may have at the time forgotten you had prayed.

Focus for today

When you pray a seemingly meaningless prayer, add a reminder to yourself of what you prayed for. Later in the day, you may find that you have reason to thank God.

Prayer

God, who answers the prayers we have already forgotten, thank you for being involved in our lives. Thank you for listening to our pleas. Thank you for not holding it against us when we forget to acknowledge you. Amen.

DAY 34 † SATURDAY

How has God touched your life this week?

How does God use you to restore people's dignity and give them hope?

Why do you sometimes miss the point when Jesus facilitates healing in someone else's life?

How has taking note of your prayers and God's answers shaped the way you recognize God's hand at work?

DAY 35 † MONDAY

Jesus, who heals our enemies

🕊 Read Luke 22:50-51

*J*ESUS SAYS, "'LOVE YOUR ENEMIES, do good to those who hate you, bless those who curse you, pray for those who abuse you'" (Luke 6:27-28). He practices what he preaches. By doing so, he goes beyond the general expectation. To many Jews of Jesus' day, good comes to those who do good, and evil comes to those who do evil. Their frame of reference never included the thought that you could *bless* those who sought your downfall. Jesus breaks the power of retribution, vengeance, and hate. He could have succumbed to the belief of many that the high priest's guard somehow deserved what was coming to him. But Jesus loves even those who choose to oppose him; he does good to those who plot against him.

What impact does this event have on the life of the person who struck the servant? John's Gospel names Peter as the one who drew the sword, but Luke does not name the offender. "No more of this!" Jesus commands. Can Jesus speak these words of healing into our lives today? Can Jesus transform our thoughts of anger, resentment, revenge, and violence into emotions that will facilitate healing—not only for us but also for those who oppose us? "No more of this!"

Do we use our devotion to God as an excuse to hurt others? "No more of this!" Jesus Christ does not ask his followers to pursue every possible means to advance their own interests. Jesus-followers walk the path of peace and of healing. Read through the passage again. See the sword in your own hand. Name the high priest's servant. Hear Jesus speak and touch despite your fear and anger. Drop your sword to the ground. "No more of this!"

Reflection

Anger and resentment have a snowball effect. The more you dwell on these thoughts and feelings, the larger they grow. These feelings can demolish the good that exists within you. Today's miracle emphasizes the power of love over the power of animosity. Which of these emotions shapes your life?

Focus for today

You may choose to make that dreaded phone call, seeking reconciliation with someone who has been a threat to your well-being. When faced with the option to act, think, and speak in violence, remember Jesus' words: "No more of this!"

Prayer

Healer of our enemies, we pray for our own healing. Change our attitudes, our thoughts, our actions, and our words so that we will not seek the path of destruction but will learn from you the way of peace, love, and healing. May we practice what you preached. Amen.

THE GOSPEL OF JOHN

Getting to Know Jesus Who Brings Life

*J*OHN TAKES A PHILOSOPHICAL approach in telling the Jesus-story. Rich in imagery, John's account uses illustrations to proclaim that Jesus is God and that the life Jesus brings is available to all. John describes the miracles as signs. These signs point to the reality of God's presence. God resides with the people. By reading through these last miracles and preparing for this holy weekend, journey with God, who is truly present with you.

DAY 36 † TUESDAY

Jesus, who saves each moment

🕊 Read John 2:1-11

KARL BARTH, A TWENTIETH-CENTURY Swiss theologian states the following: "God . . . makes good what we do badly."[3] Today we focus on what God can do within our controllable situations. The lack of sufficient wine for the wedding guests as described in the text is a serious matter. Wedding feasts in Jesus' time and culture lasted much longer than the weddings and receptions that we know in the Western context. It was not unusual for a wedding feast to last for a week with guests arriving and departing during the course of festivities.

Gauging the amount of wine and food for such an event was a daunting task. In this situation the person responsible calculates incorrectly. Someone has to assume the blame. Can you imagine being that person—whether the groom or the steward of the feast? The situation must have caused great embarrassment. Apologies may have dominated the conversations. We can even hear this person thinking, *Is there any hope, any solution to this problem?* We can sense the relief when he discovers that more wine has miraculously appeared—not only wine but good wine!

This parable speaks to far more than Jesus' ability to turn water into wine. It speaks about God's activity within the domain of our responsibilities. God makes good what we do badly. This does not absolve us from carrying out our tasks to the best of our ability. However, where we face brokenness and failure, even in our best attempts, we rest assured that God is at work. We can always bring our responsibilities to God, even if we know that what we have planned and what we have done may not suffice. Then we dare pray, "God, please make good what we did badly."

Reflection

Recall an event where your best was simply not good enough. How did you experience God's presence in that situation?

Focus for today

Look over your journal or list of things to do. Take note of your responsibilities for today. You hope to do your best in each activity. Lift these plans up to God, so that if need be, God may make good what you do badly.

Prayer

Almighty God, we confess that we are not you; therefore, we cannot do everything perfectly. Today we pledge to do our best in all things and ask that you transform our lives into lives of worship, lives good and pleasing to you. Heal us, we pray, from the belief that we act beyond your transforming influence. Amen.

DAY 37 † WEDNESDAY

Jesus, who redeems when all seems lost

🕊 Read John 4:46-54

*T*HE FINAL VERSES of this passage suggest that the official and his family come to believe as a result of the miracle. The official, however, must have been inclined to believe that Jesus could perform such a wonder. According to John, this is the second miracle that took place or, in his words, "the second sign." What does Jesus want to reveal by giving this "sign"? The official's voice may betray his desperation. Perhaps he risks everything—professional and personal credibility and integrity—by trying to get a miracle from the one who turned water into wine.

I think that the official comes to Jesus as a last hope, the final attempt at saving his son's life. The news of the miracle at Cana has traveled, and this man learns of one with powers beyond that of an ordinary human. When Jesus restores his son's health, the lives of both the official and those of his household are changed.

We may feel ashamed to admit that we lift up prayers of desperation as well. We have found ourselves in situations where we have tried absolutely everything, keeping God in the background. Then when all else failed, we resorted to prayer. It is part of our human frailty to exhaust all options and then to give God a try. This was not the official's motive, but we recognize the trend of our using God as a last option.

"Lord, I know I didn't study hard enough, but please help me pass this exam." "Lord, I have tried everything. I give up. Only you can pull this one out of the fire." Do these words sound familiar? The amazing aspect of this account is that Jesus acts even in our desperation. He does not respond with words such as these: "Well, why didn't you come to me in the first place?" or "Seeing that you wanted to do everything on your own, I am washing my hands of you." No, Jesus acts in grace.

Of course, Jesus won't write our exams for us or suddenly deposit a huge amount of money into our bank accounts, but Jesus works in ways that bring life to our situations of impending disaster. The sign performed demonstrates that Jesus has the power of life, a sign that will be shown in all its fullness in his own resurrection. All hope is not lost. Jesus does not turn his back on the desperate. What good news this is for us today!

Reflection

Our culture's child-rearing practices foster independence. We grow up learning to take care of ourselves and rely on no one. We seek to require no assistance in life. How free do you feel to turn to God when situations do not seem to work out?

Focus for today

Give God all of your life before you try to take control. Even in your moments of desperation, do not hesitate to turn to the one who turned water into wine.

Prayer

Jesus, in desperation we pray. Touch our lives today and help us to believe. Amen.

DAY 38 † THURSDAY

Jesus, who gets us to move

🕊 Read John 5:1-9

'D O YOU WANT TO BE MADE WELL?'" What a cutting question! The man's answer surprises. Instead of replying with an emphatic yes, he resorts to excuses for not having been healed. He sits at the edge of the pool that promotes healing. He has been here for a long time but never manages to get into the water on time. How long have we been sitting at the edge of healing, forgiveness, or reconciliation?

By being there on the edge, we display our desire for these transformations. But when Jesus asks if we want to be made well, we easily reply, "Lord, every time I want to, they . . . disappoint me, fail to come to my rescue, hurt me again." Jesus does not ask us to list our reasons for *not* being healed; he asks whether we want to be healed!

Jesus turns to the man and instructs him to stand up, take his mat, and walk. Sometimes our excuses allow us to sit on the sidelines. Our call comes in the command that we take action with regard to our situations. Are you struggling with addictions? Well, stand up and receive help. Do you suffer from estranged relationships? Stand up and make a phone call. Do you face unforgiveness? Stand up and seek forgiveness. We may linger poolside no longer, feeding off the pity of passersby.

The sick man listens. Finally, someone sees through his excuses and calls forth his potential. When he listens and obeys, he discovers the healing he has sought all along.

Friends, as we contemplate this miracle, let us consider some of the following questions: Where is our pool of Beth-zatha? Why do we choose to linger there? Is Jesus calling us to take action and experience a miracle today? Listen to his voice! He knows our capabilities and the place of our healing. Sometimes the miracles we chase are less complicated than we thought. Perhaps they require a little humility, a bit of effort, a decision to stop blaming others, and to be obedient to Jesus' instructions.

Reflection

The meditation raises some pointed questions. Name your "illness." Identify the place where you have sought comfort but not transformation. Who have you blamed for your lack of progress? What is Jesus saying to you?

Focus for today

Speak to someone about anything that bothers you—physical illness or any bad habits that have taken hold of your life. Do you desire deliverance but blame others for your condition rather than taking responsibility? Allow God to speak through others.

Prayer

We cannot hide anything from you, O God of truth. Our excuses debilitate us. Our excuses become the truth for our lives. Jesus, we want to be healed. Heal us from our inability to see what a difference it can make to receive help, to talk to those estranged from us, or decide to work toward wholeness in relationships. Amen.

DAY 39 † GOOD FRIDAY

Jesus, who takes away the blame

🌱 Read John 9:1-7

Whose fault was it?" What an appropriate question for Good Friday. This question assumes that God blesses the righteous and curses the wicked. Our first son, Matthew, was born with a congenital heart defect. My wife and I did not know about these problems before his birth but were surprised by these facts minutes after he took his first breath. Whose fault was it? Who was to blame for this suffering of the innocent? These questions tortured us and our families as we tried to make sense of our new journey.

I'm sure the parents of the man born blind raised the same questions at his birth. Many people back then (and even now) believe that illness and disability represent God's anger toward an individual. The religious leaders at the Temple may have conveyed the belief that the man would never merit God's love or be accepted as an equal in fellowship with others.

Imagine this man conversing with himself, saying, "I wish I were the same as. . . . " He not only desires to see but to know that God doesn't hold a grudge against him or his family. It is a familiar story. It is our story. We can all recall a time when we did not feel that we or our loved ones merited God's affection.

Then Jesus utters words of healing: "Neither this man nor his parents . . . " Another miracle takes place: theologies and perspectives change. The man receives his sight and the confirmation that God is not angry with him. The Cross offers a statement of wholeness. Jesus, the innocent one, suffered; but God did not abandon us. God continues to love us; God loves us still.

Reflection

You may acknowledge the fact that your need for vengeance often skews your sense of justice. We, like the people in Jesus' time, think that innocent suffering serves as God's way of bringing about justice. What parallels do you see between this story and the story of the Cross?

Focus for today

God is not angry with you. This is a statement of salvation! Even when those who crucified Jesus tried their best to get rid of him, God did not retaliate in vengeance or anger. Let this truth speak to your life.

Prayer

Jesus, as we look upon the Cross and mourn your death, we ask the question: "Whose fault is it?" Then you speak, O God, catching us off guard with the pronouncement that we are to blame no longer. We thank you for your love. Amen.

DAY 40 † SATURDAY

Jesus, who rolls stones away

🐚 Read John 11:1-44

*D*EATH IS SO FINAL, isn't it? We associate the term *death* with our own mortality and also use it to describe situations that we deem to be beyond hope, beyond salvation. "My relationship is dead." "Hope is dead." "My future is dead." The raising of Lazarus involves more than Jesus' returning his friend to life. It describes our encounter with what we have written off. Both Mary and Martha express the prayer we often pray, "Lord, if you had been here, my brother would not have died." Our prayers stop here. Martha surprises us. She adds, "But even now I know that God will give you whatever you ask of him."

The people move to the tomb and when Jesus orders the stone to be rolled away, Martha returns to her logic: "But, Lord, he has been dead for days! There will be a terrible stench!" (AP). Jesus proceeds to call Lazarus by name, and Lazarus comes out.

Imagine standing before the tomb of that which you deem beyond repair. When Jesus orders the stone to be rolled away, what part of you calls out to Jesus saying, "It's hopeless!" This day we let go of our assumptions of perceived finality—we release our hopelessness and let Jesus stand before that tomb with us. Then we discover that the relationship, hope, or future that we had written off is called to life by the One who knows no limitations.

Reflection

As you move toward the day of Resurrection, Jesus inspires life in you. What relationship, dream, or situation in your life needs resurrection?

Focus for today

Mourn the things that have passed from your life, but do not give up hope that it is possible to be raised from the dead. This is Easter's proclamation.

Prayer

The tomb is occupied. The stone is in place, not to be moved. Lord, when you command the stone to be rolled away, may life spring forth in newness. Amen.

- How have you experienced God's ability to make good what you have done badly?

- What action do you need to take to participate in the process of your own healing?

- Who do you blame for your experiences of brokenness?

- Why should you take the risk of allowing Jesus to stand before the tomb of that which you have buried?

EASTER SUNDAY

Jesus, who is Lord

🌫 Read John 21:1-11

*I*T IS THE LORD!" "It must be the Lord, for no one else commands such authority!" Have you ever uttered words like these? Can you remember your exhilaration when realizing that God was present and acting in the moment when you least expected anything to transpire?

The disciples feel fatigued. They can no longer continue. Dawn is breaking; a night filled with disappointment lay behind them. They have returned to their "before-Jesus" vocations. Not only do they return, but they have nothing to show for it.

Then Jesus stands on the banks and again calls them to follow him. He's back! This scripture offers another Resurrection reflection—the story of Easter all over again. It is the story of all that seems lost and meaningless, much like the disciples' experience of the Crucifixion. And then, like Mary's realization on Easter Sunday comes the recognition, the proclamation: "It is the Lord!" This is the miracle: those who find themselves tossed and turned by disappointment can look up and be filled with the joy and ecstasy of recognizing Jesus! Despair turns to hope. Dismay turns to the belief that all is not lost. Downcast eyes look up, and tears of sorrow become tears of relief.

The following texts come to life in this event: "'I am the bread of life. Whoever comes to me will never be hungry'" (John 6:35); "'Come to me, all you that are weary and are carrying heavy burdens, and I will give you rest'" (Matt. 11:28); "'Peace I leave with you; my peace I give to you. I do not give to you as the world gives. Do not let your hearts be troubled, and do not let them be afraid'" (John 14:27). Have you witnessed this miracle lately?

Reflection

What a glorious moment as we recognize Jesus' voice when all seems to be lost. Our own efforts are not enough. We are weary of being battered and bruised by relying only on our own strength. Jesus invites us to approach matters in a different way. Jesus comes to change our life.

Focus for today

As you journey through the Easter weekend, recognize the change that Jesus brings to people's lives. Celebrate this as you remind yourself that despite Friday and the death we remember, Sunday is coming, filled with hope, joy, and new life.

Prayer

Resurrected Lord, our best efforts leave us feeling tired and forlorn. Call out to us. Speak to us about things we need to do differently. When we obey, we will know that the goodness that follows is not because of us but because "It is the Lord!" Amen.

AN OUTLINE FOR SMALL-GROUP USE

Here is a simple plan for a one-hour, weekly group meeting based on reading *The Miracles of Jesus*. One person may act as convener every week, or the role can rotate among group members. You may want to light a white Christ candle each week to signal the beginning of your time together.

OPENING

Convener: Let us come into the presence of God.
Others: Lord Jesus Christ, thank you for being with us. May we hear your word to us as we speak to one another.

SCRIPTURE

Convener reads one of the scriptures suggested for that week in *The Miracles of Jesus*. After a one- or two-minute silence, convener asks: What did you hear God saying to you in this passage? What response does this call for? (Group members respond in turn or as led.)

REFLECTION

- What scripture passage(s) and meditation(s) from this week was (were) particularly meaningful for you? Why? (Group members respond in turn or as led.)

- What actions were you nudged to take in response to the week's meditations? (Group members respond in turn or as led.)

- Where were you challenged in your discipleship this week? How did you respond to the challenge? (Group members respond in turn or as led.)

PRAYING TOGETHER

Convener says: Based on today's discussion, what people and situations do you want us to pray for now and in the coming week? Convener or other volunteer then prays about the concerns named.

DEPARTING

Convener says: Let us go in peace to serve God and our neighbors in all that we do.

Adapted from *The Upper Room* daily devotional guide, January–February 2001. © 2000 The Upper Room. Used by permission.

NOTES

1. George Arthur Buttrick, ed., *The Interpreter's Bible: The Holy Scriptures in the King James and Revised Standard Versions with General Articles and Introduction, Exegesis, Exposition for Each Book of the Bible*, vol. 7: The Gospel According to St. Matthew, The Gospel According to St. Mark (New York: Abingdon-Cokesbury Press, 1951), 668.

2. "John Wesley's Explanatory Notes, Mark 9" http://www.christnotes.org/commentary. php?com=wes&b=41&c=9.

3. Karl Barth, *Church Dogmatics: The Doctrine of the Word of God*, vol. 1, part 2, trans. G. T. Thomson and Harold Knight (Edinburgh: T. & T. Clark Ltd, 1956), 751.

ABOUT THE AUTHOR

Rev. Dr. Wessel Bentley is Chief Researcher at the Research Institute for Theology and Religion (University of South Africa). He is an ordained minister in the Methodist Church of Southern Africa. Wessel, his wife, and two sons live in Pretoria.

Wessel is the author of two books in the 28 Days of Prayer series: *Facing Financial Struggle* and *Praying through a Child's Illness*. He also authored *The Notion of Mission in Karl Barth's Ecclesiology*, and he edited *What Are We Thinking?* and *Methodism in Southern Africa*. His research interests are Christology, Ecclesiology, Science and Religion, and Church-State relationships.

Follow Wessel on Twitter @wesselbentley.